Holaku's Return

A Four-Act Play

To watch the play, please scan the following QR Code:
Holaku's Return

Dr. Sultan bin Muhammad Al-Qasimi

Holaku's Return

A Four-Act Play

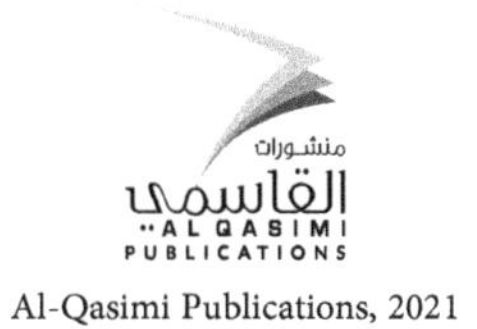

Al-Qasimi Publications, 2021

Book Title: Holaku's Return (A Four-Act Play)
First published in 1998 in Arabic as "Eawdat Hulaku"
by: Al-Qasimi Publications
Author: Dr. Sultan bin Muhammad Al-Qasimi (United Arab Emirates)
Publisher Name: Al-Qasimi Publications
Sharjah, United Arab Emirates
Edition: Second
Year of publication: 2021

ISBN: 978-9948-02-42-55
Printing Permission: National Media Council, Abu Dhabi, UAE
No. MC 01-03-4017683, Date: 05-08-2021

Age Classification: E
The age group that matches the content of the books was classified according to the age classification issued by the National Council for Media
----
Al- Qasimi Publications, Al Tarfa, Sheikh Mohammed Bin Zayed Road
PO Box 64009 Sharjah, United Arab Emirates
Tel: 0097165090000, Fax: 0097165520070
Email: info@aqp.ae

CONTENTS

Prologue

The Abbasid Caliphate-Kingdom-was the third of the Islamic Caliphates to succeed the Islamic Prophet Mohammad during 750-1258- C.E (132-656 Hijri). It was golden age of Islamic civilization and culture.

Through my in-depth study of the history of the Arab nations, I have come to the conclusion that the circumstances that brought about the downfall of the Abbasid Kingdom-Caliphate in 1258 C.E (750A.H) are quite similar to what is happening now in the Arab world.

In other words history is repeating itself. I, therefore, wrote this play "Holaku's Return" with a Historical perspective to stage a painful reality.

All the incidents, places and names of characters

in this play are authentic and every term mentioned in this text is a real indicator that elucidates what is happening in the Arab nations.

Dr. Sultan bin Muhammad Al Qasimi

Historical Background

Genghis Khan (died 1227 AD)

In 1215 AD the great Mongol leader Genghis Khan took peking and as lord of China advanced westward to secure the flow of trade. After two failed missions, in 1220 Geghis Khan overrun the Iranian Empire of Khorasan, at that time being under the rule of the Khwarezm-Shah dynasty (11th - 13th century), and comprising a vast territory which extended from Chinese Turkistan in the east to the borders of Iraq in the west. Bukhara, Samarkand, Heart and other cities were completely destroyed, the population massacred.

Holaku: (c. 1217 - 1265)

A second Mongol invasion began with Holaku (Arab. Name of Hulegu), a grandson of Genghis Khan. Together with his brother Mongke, the heir to the great Mongol empire, he set out in about 1253 with a Mongol army of about 130,000 and launched an attack on Iran. Holaku crushed the last resistance there by the end of 1256, when he destroyed the assassin fortress at Alamut.

The Assassin (an Ismailite sect) where the product of dynastic strife among the Fatamids, who were the heads of the Shiite Ismailite movement and had set up a rival Caliphate in Egypt in opposition to that of the Abbasids in Baghdad. After the death of Fatimid Caliph Al Mustansir (1094), Hassan -e- Sabah, the Assassin leader, and other Ismailities in Iran refused to recognize the new Fatimid caliph in Cairo and transferred their allegiance to his deposed elder brother Nizar. There thus grew up the sect of the Nizari Ismailites, who were at odds with the Fatimid caliphs in Cairo and were also deeply hostile to the Abbasids. In 1090 Hassan and his followers had captured the hill fortress of Alamut near Qazvin in Iran. The following 150 years the Assassin leaders commanded from this stronghold a network of propagandists in Iran, Iraq and later Syria, a corps of devoted suicide attackers and an unknown number of agents. Soon the Assassin was claiming many victims among the generals and statesmen of the Abbasid Caliphate, including two caliphs. Assassin power came to an end as the Mongols under Holaku captured Assassin's castles in Iran one by one until 1256 Alamut itself fell.

Holaku captured all Iran and made it his base. He founded the Il-Khanid dynasty (1256-1339) there and attacked the Abbasid Caliphate (750-1258).

In 1258 Holaku besieged Baghdad, where divided counsels prevented the city's salvation. Al Mustasim (r. 1242-1258), the last Abbasid caliph of Baghdad, had presented no strong defence against the Mongols conqueror. He had ignored several demands of Holaku and had answered others with blustering and empty threats. When Holaku entered Baghdad, the Caliph and 300 officials hurried to present their surrender, but were all executed. Baghdad was largely destroyed and thousands of its inhabitants were killed. Thereafter Baghdad became the provincial capital of the Il-Khanids.

Holaku hoped to extend the Mongol empire as far as the Mediterranean. In 1259 the Mongol army moved into Syria, took Aleppo and Damascus, and reached the shore of Mediterranean sea. The Mongols then sent an envoy to Cairo in 1260 to demand the submission of the Mumluk Sultan, whose reply was the execution of the envoy. The Mongol army was lured into a trap at Ayn Jalut, in Palestine, by a Mumluk force and completely destroyed. After the Mumluk victory the Mongols were also driven out of Syria. Holaku was unable to take reprisals, as he was preoccupied with internal power struggles. Thus Holaku returned to Iran. The Il-Khanid dynasty reunited Iran as a political and territorial entity. It made Azerbaijan its centre and established Tabriz as its first capital until Sultaniyeh was built early in the 14th century. Soon after that the rule of the Il-Khanids came to an end.

Main Characters

in order of their appearance

- **Al Mustasim,** Chief of the Abbasids, Caliph of Baghdad
- **Al Duwaidar Al Sageer,** Army Commander of the Caliph
- **Ibn Al Algami,** Minister of the Caliph
- **Porter 1,** at the court of the Caliph
- **Youths,** Protest Leader from Baghdad
- **Porter 2,** at the Court of the Caliph
- **Al Sharabi,** Senior Officer of the Caliph
- **Several Soldiers,** at the Court of the Caliph
- **Holaku,** Mongol Leader, grandson of Genghis Khan
- **Officer 1,** Serviceman of Holaku
- **Envoy,** Serviceman of Holaku
- **Officer 2,** Serviceman of Holaku

- **Porter,** Attendant of Holaku
- **Rukn Al Deen Khorshah,** One of the Ismailities, a Muslim faction
- **Several Ministers,** Followers of Rukn Al Deen
- **Guard,** Serviceman of Holaku
- **Totar,** Commander of Holaku
- **Officer,** Serviceman of Holaku
- **The Dartanki,** Military Commissioner of the Caliph
- **Porter 3,** at the Court of the Caliph
- **Abu Al Abbas,** Son of Al Mustasim, the Caliph
- **Porter 4,** at the Court of the Caliph
- **Several Soldiers,** Servicemen of Holaku
- **Prince,** Mongol Governor of Baghdad after its fall
- **Noble men,** Citizens of Baghdad
- **Officer,** Attendant of Ibn Al Algami
- **Several soldiers,** Serviceman of Holaku
- **New Minister,** Son of Ibn Al Algami
- **One man,** Citizen of Baghdad

ACT 1

Period:

Year 633 Hijri, 1255 AD

Location:

Baghdad

The Caliph Al Mustasim, the minister of Ibn Al Algami, the Army Commander Al Duwaidar Al Sageer; all are assembling at the Caliph's Council.

Al Mustasim: Duwaidar, our army commander. What is the news on Mongols?

Al Duwaidar: My Lord they are surrounding three Muslim forts in ton, Truksheez and kamly and none of the Muslims dares to help them. It is really disappointing.

Al Mustasim: And you Ibn Al Algami, our minister! What news do you have on Mongols?

Ibn Al Algami: My Lord, it is said that Holaku, the commander of the Mongol army, has already reached those forts.

A porter enters with a message

Porter: My Lord, a messenger from Holaku has just arrived with this message.

Ibn Al Algami receives the message

Al Mustasim: Read the message!

**** The Hijri date corresponds to the year 622 of the Gregorian calendar which is the year of the emigration of the Prophet Mohammad from Makkah to Madinah.***

Ibn Al Algami starts reading the message

Al Algami: My Lord, Holaku asks you to send a battalion to join in his war against the Muslim forts which are surrounded by his forces.

Al Mustasim: What do you think Ibn Al Algami?

Ibn Al Algami: My Lord, I think we better send the battalion.

Al Mustasim: I am also thinking of the same.

Al Duwaidar: I am against sending a battalion to join in this war.

Ibn Al Algami: addressing Al Duwaidar, Firstly those people are of different conception and inclination. Secondly they represent a great danger to the area. Didn't you hear about the long list of victims who were brutally murdered by those people? Why do we blame the Mongols in their siege of the forts? Don't you remember those forts were once pockets of terrorism in the Mongol's lands, threatening both the Mongols security and Mongol leaders?

Al Duwaidar: I agree with you, Ibn Al Algami. But Holako doesn't need this assistance. He is fox like and he wants to see the soldiers moving out so that he can capture Baghdad easily.

Al Mustasim: What do you think Al Duwaidar?

Al Duwaidar: Send him some gifts instead of soldiers.

Exit Al Duwaidar leaving Al Mustasim with his minister.

Al Mustasim addresses Ibn Al Algami

Al Mustasim: Come on … write a message to Holaku!

Ibn Al Algami gets ready holding a paper and a pen and Al Mustasim tries to dictate.

Al Mustasim: Write down …. Write down …

Ibn Al Algami: My Lord, Let me write the message!

He starts writing thereby reading what he writes.

From the Abbasid Caliph Al Mustasim Abdulla Ibn Al Mustansir to the Great Holaku. Would you please forgive me, I regret inability to dispatch any army to support you.

Here the Caliph becomes excited.

The Caliph: I am Abbasid Caliph! How can I so degrade myself to this infidel?

Ibn Al Algami: My Lord! It is just ink on paper, nobody will see it and Duwaidar is not attending to object or refuse these words.

Al Mustasim: Alright, Ibn Al Algami go ahead and complete the message!

Ibn Al Algami completes the message and hands it over to Al Mustasim, who reads and signs it. He then rises to remove a carpet revealing a number of boxes filled up with jewels, opens them one by one and selects some jewels to send to Holaku. He seems hesitant while giving Ibn Al Algami each collection.

Al Mustasim: No, no.... this is too much .... Only this, not this ...not this, only this, yes only this enough!

Ibn Al Algami: My Lord, you have a great deal of these jewels and nothing would diminish from these boxes! You are fending of an evil!

Al Mustasim: All these jewels and money are guarantee of this Caliphate.

Exits Ibn Al Algami carrying the message and the jewels.

Enters Al Mustasim into the house where women laughter, giggles and songs are heard.

Suddenly there are voices at the door and a porter is trying to stop a group of youths from getting in.

The porter enters the Caliph's room together with the group.

One of the Youths: We want to see Sharabi, the senior officer of the Royal Palace.

The Porter: He is inside with the Caliph.

The group of youths makes noises. Enters Sharabi from the direction of the Caliph's House.

Al Sharabi: What is this noise? Who are you and what do you want?

One of the Youths: We are a group of Muslims; we have come to see the Caliph.

Al Sharabi: The Caliph is busy now!

Hear women's giggles and music.

Youth: Nobody caused affliction to this nation other than you as you are the one responsible for selecting this weak Caliph. You are the one, who makes him indulge in pleasure with women, dance and fun so that you can dominate and overpower the machinery of government. When many of the Abbasid people refused the selection of this Caliph, you were the one who exposed them to torture and punishment and threw them into prisons just to have their recognition by force.

Al Sharabi: Get out of here, The Caliph doesn't want to see anyone!

Youths voices become louder

Caliph: from inside

Al Sharabi: who is there with you?

Al Sharabi: My Lord, it's a group of rabble-rousers!

Caliph: Kick them out, Sharabi!

Sharabi forces the youths out assisted by some armed soldiers.

Women's giggles and music become louder.

CURTAIN DROP
END OF ACT 1

ACT 2

Scene:

Maymoon's fort in Bastam which lies to the north of Persia. Residence of Rukn Al Deen Khorshah, the faction chieftain.

Holaku has set up the tent in front of the fort.

Holaku seems roaring as he is sending a last messenger to Rukn Al Deen Khorshah.

Holaku: Maymoon's fort has made me crazy! It is still hard to break through! We have surrounded it for a long time in vain and now winter is coming with its snow and severe cold.

One of Holaku's men: My Lord, let us wait for the reply.

Holaku: I had sent him mission after mission and a delegate after another, in no less than eight occasions, sometimes asking him to submit through promise of wealth and fortune, at others informing him on the grief and destruction, he would face, if he chooses not to, but all in vain.

Holaku to his envoy.

Holaku: Go to Rukn Al Deen Khorshah and in my name give him a guarantee for his life and also for that of his followers.

The envoys move to the fort.

Holaku: turning to his leaders, What about the other forts?

One Leader: They are still resisting, we have been surrounding some forts for a whole year and they could remain firm for another twenty years.

Holaku: Stay on it! Bring me the drinks and the dancing girls … quick!

Drink is brought and Mongolian music is heard. All people are looking towards the stage where shadows of dancing girls are seen.

A porter enters shouting

Porter: My Lord! My Lord! The fort has fallen!

The music stops and once again the porter shouts

Porter: The fort has fallen and Rukn Al Deen Khorshah and his followers are coming with the envoys.

Holaku: with a sigh of pleasure

Splendid! Splendid!

For a while Holaku dances with his followers and with disgrace enters Rukn Al Deen Khorshah in his Islamic dress. Holaku welcomes him and makes him sit beside him.

Holaku: Come on; bring Mongol lass for Rukn Al Deen Khorshah. Now we want you to co-operate with us to stop the bloodshed.

Rukn Al Deen: Please.

Holaku: I would like you to send your delegates to instruct your troops in all the fortified forts to give up.

Rukn Al Deen: to his ministers, Come on. Let everyone of you, accompanied by a squad from Holaku's army, go there and ask submission in my name.

Rukn Al Deen's ministers exit.

Holaku: turning to one of his guards, Did you bring the Mongol lass?

The Guard: Yes, my Lord, she is inside.

Holaku: addressing Rukn Al Deen, Welcome my dear and have a happy night with your wife!

Enters Rukn Al Deen Khorshah to a side of the theatre, while Holaku stays.

Mongolian music is played, lights gradually starts to fade. After complete darkness, lights appear again showing Rukn Al Deen sitting inside the tent.

Enters one of his followers, called Jowaini, greeting Rukn Al Deen.

Rukn Al Deen: Mercy and blessing of Allah be upon you! Come on, Jowaini tell me what the news is!

Jowaini: My lord, all the forts gave up and surrendered! All peoples seemed annoyed and displeased with you. My Lord, you are in great danger.

Rukn Al Deen: This is the result of Al Tusi's plotting, who has been seeking only for his personal interests. By him I was convinced of the surrender and now he will accompany Mongols to Baghdad.

Enters Holaku roaring.

Holaku: Hello my dear friend! I hope you had a happy night with your Mongal wife.

**** Naseer Al Tusi, philosopher and mathematician. He espoused the faith of the Ismailite sect, accepted however immediately after the fall of Baghdad a position with the Mongols as a scientific advisor. The topic of whether Al Tusi accompanied the Mongol capture of Baghdad remains controversial.***

Rukn Al Deen: Your Majesty! I hope you would release me from going with you and send me with this wife to Mongol land.

Holaku: As you like, my dear! You have achieved our mission in peace. Please!

Pointing to one direction in the theatre.

Exit Rukn Al Deen with Al Jowaini.

Holaku turns to the commander Totar.

Holaku: Commander Totar, send Rukn Al Deen Khorshah to the Mongol land.

Pointing to his neck with a sign that means execution.

Enters one of Holaku's officers carrying a message.

Officer: My Lord! This is the Abbasid Caliph message. He refuses the idea of sending his forces to join our wars against the forts.

Holaku laughs scornfully while he dances.

Holaku: Hahahaha! Then let us set for Baghdad to punish him.

Holaku swings hid swords and exits shouting

Baghdad! Baghdad! Power is rightness and that is our everlasting slogan.

CURTAIN DROP
END OF ACT 2

ACT 3

Scene:

The Abbasid Caliph's Palace (As in Act 1)

Al Mustasim: Duwaidar, what is Holaku's news?

Al Duwaidar: My Lord, he has reached Hamdhan.

Al Mustasim: He hasn't answered our message.

Ibn Al Algami: He captured all the fortified forts, so there is no need of our help.

Al Duwaidar: It was by disgrace and violations that he succeeded to occupy these forts.

Someone knocks at the door, enters a porter with a message.

Porter: A message from Holaku.

Al Duwaidar receives the message.

Al Mustasim: Come on, read it over, Duwaidar!

Duwaidar starts reading the message.

Al Duwaidar: From Holaku to Al Mustasim! We have sent you our delegates at a time when we set to conquer the Malahda forts. We asked you to provide us with soldiers. Although you had displayed loyalty, you didn't send the soldiers to support us. The real indication of loyalty and support is to carry out our orders and send us your army to back us against those tyrants, but you did not send the army offering hollow and false pretexts.

Nevertheless, if you carry out orders, everything will be completely forgotten. You have to demolish the forts, fill up with earth all the trenches around Baghdad, pass the country administration to your son and present yourself against us. Failing to do that and unwilling to come, you better send your minister and the army commander to inform you with no more and no less of our final message.

Al Mustasim: in a state of anger, I am the Abbasid Caliph! Do I have to take orders from this stupid....! Come on, Ibn Al Algami and write down. Holaku I warn you and your soldiers of Gods Humiliation, if you subject and oppose the Abbasid people. All Muslims from the east to west are at my back and call. They will be under my command against the invaders, the Mongol.

Al Duwaidar looking at the roof, turning his eyes, tapping with fingers at Al Mustasim's pretension while Ibn Al Algami is swinging his head left and right, looking at Al Mustasim and using his hands and fingers as a sign, asking him to tone down.

Al Mustasim: Write down...., Despite all this Islamic power I am unwilling to use it as I do not want to upset those Muslims and cause any disturbance by this war. Holaku! I advise you, you should think of peace and withdraw! Otherwise I ask you to drawback to Khurasan and we will give you our concessions of all the lands you have occupied with our consent and satisfaction to annex them to the Mongol lands.

Al Mustasim: looking at Ibn Al Algami, Did you write? We will renounce the lands that you have occupied. Annex them to the Mongol land so that peace will prevail between us.

Al Mustasim signs the message stamps it and hands it over to Ibn Al Algami.

Al Mustasim: Now send this message with some gifts to Holaku.

Exits Ibn Al Algami while Al Duwaidar remains with Al Mustasim.

Al Duwaidar: My Lord, is this true?

Al Mustasim: True? It is not true, but how Holaku was made aware of our situation?

Al Duwaidar: How? First through your minister and those, whom he had appointed to look after his interests.

Al Mustasim: My minister? I don't believe this! Hahaha!

Al Duwaidar: My lord, for two years I kept asking you to provide us with enough money to build a strong army worth of defending you and Islam! What did you benefit from all these jewels that you accumulate and heaped up? I had asked you to submit this case to the Muslim leaders hoping every one of them would bear the responsibility, but you didn't listen to me and listened only to Ibn Al Algami's words.

Enters Ibn Al Algami.

Ibn Al Algami: we have sent Holaku the delegate.

Exits Al Duwaidar boiling.

Ibn Al Algami: what is the matter with this man?

Al Mustasim: Don't worry! Now, tell me what shall we do to stop Holaku's march against us?

Ibn Al Algami: My Lord, we must pay out money to stop this enemy.

Al Mustasim: How is that? Like how Duwaidar suggests?

Ibn Al Algami: What does Duwaidar suggest?

Al Mustasim: Giving money for building up forces.

Ibn Al Algami: laughing, Human beings would be killed, money would be lost. My Lord, the Mongols have a great striking force with a destructive weapon that we could not face.

Al Mustasim: What is that weapon?

Ibn Al Algami: That is a catapult by which they throw igneous shells and arrows. They use Chinese experts to operate these flame-throwers.

Al Mustasim: What shall we do?

Ibn Al Algami: from a paper that he draws from his pocket, My Lord! All the money and jewels that you have were for this day to fend of this evil from this family and also to protect dignity, honor and self safety. Therefore we should prepare the following: One thousand loads of priceless gems, one thousand loads of well-bred camels, one thousand of the highly regarded Arabian horses loaded with all necessities. Offer Holaku our apology, Khutba[1] should be delivered in mosques in his names and coins should be minted with this title.

Al Mustasim: Splendid, splendid! I approve of this proper suggestion. Let these things be prepared quickly and then send them to the Mongol's leader Holaku.

Enters Al Duwaidar sneering.

1- Khutba is a sermon, delivered especially at a Friday service, at the two major Islamic festivals (Eids), and on extraordinary occasions.

Al Duwaidar: Allah! Allah! You have it all out, Ibn Al Algami.

Ibn Al Algami: What do you mean?

Al Duwaidar: The conspiracy, you betrayer, own interest seeker, wooing Holaku's friendship!

Ibn Al Algami: I refuse this charge.

Al Duwaider: I swear I would, personally and with my men, challenge and confiscate these gifts and arrest all delegates and attendants of this campaign.

Al Mustasim: appeasing Al Duwaidar, Fine... Fine... As you like we will send Al Dartanki with some gifts as well.

Al Duwaidar: What does this Dartanki do? Only going to Holaku, to and fro?

Ibn Al Algami: Before you leave, what mockery did you make? Why did you send forces to murder and plunder the people of Alkarkh, while we were living in distress? If you were bold enough, face the Mongols and not those unarmed people!

Ibn Al Algami turns to Al Mustasim and continues.

My Lord, even your son was taking part in this conspiracy.

Al Mustasim: Now get out! Leave me alone!

Exit Al Duwaidar followed by Ibn Al Algami.

The Caliph: Oh my Lord, I am really puzzled between Al Algami and Duwaidar!

Al Mustasim keeps silent, light gradually starts to dim till complete darkness.

A voice comes from the coulisse.

Voice: And the day pass by.

Al Mustasim sitting in his royal court. Ibn Al Algami is attending; Enters Al Duwaidar dragging Al Dartanki with the gift box.

Al Duwaidar: Take this Dartanki with all your gifts and money!

Al Mustasim: Dartanki, what is the matter?

Al Dartanki: My Lord, I was kicked out with this message from Holaku asking you to present yourself before him if you wish to become a subordinate governor to the Mongols. Otherwise you must promptly send him the minister Ibn Al Algami, the army commander Duwaidar and his deputy Suleiman Shah.

Ibn Al Algami: Splendid, all of us will go!

Al Mustasim: I agree. Let all of you go there?

Al Duwaidar: looking at Al Mustasim,Who is going to command the forces and defend Baghdad? Holaku wants to imprison me with Suleiman Shah or kill both of us. So the army would find no one to command it.

Al Mustasim: That is right.

Enters a porter shouting.

Porter: My Lord! Holaku's forces are surrounding Baghdad.

Al Mustasim: There is neither might nor power except from All the most High, the Greatest. Now come on Duwaidar, think up and advice me!

Al Duwaidar: pointing to Ibn Al Algami, Let him proceed to Holaku, while Suleiman Shah and me will remain here with you.

Al Mustasim: to Ibn Al Algami, That is good.

Tell Holaku that I have fulfilled my promise. Now I am sending you asking his excuse for not being able to send both Duwaidar and Suleiman Shah! Come on, go!

Exits Ibn Al Algami.

Al Duwaidar asks permission from Al Mustasim to take his leave.

Al Duwaidar: Excuse me my lord! I will go to make the forces ready to defend Baghdad.

Exits Al Duwaidar, the Caliph keeps going to and fro on the stage.

The Caliph: Even if a person thinks of getting away, he will fail, for their forces are circling all of Baghdad.

After a while enters Abu Al Abbasi, Al Mustasim's son.

Abu Al Abbasi: Peace be upon you, father.

Al Mustasim: Peace be upon, my son.

Abu Al Abbasi: Father, I was informed that you have sent Ibn Al Algami to Holaku.

Al Mustasim: Yes, that is true my son.

Abu Al Abbasi: But Ibn Al Algami is still in Baghdad and the Mongols are rushing over Baghdad walls.

Al Mustasim: Now I have started suspecting Ibn Al Algami.

Abu Al Abbasi: No use, it's too late father! Repeatedly I have warned you of Ibn Al Algami.

Al Mustasim: Come on, my son take some gifts, the country's notables and officials and proceed to Holaku. Also take Ibn Al Algami with you.

Abu Al Abbasi: Again Ibn Al Algami!

Exits Abu Abbasi.

Al Mustasim remains greatly disturbed, moving to and fro.

From the scenes sounds of war and noise is heard.

Voice: The Ajami Tower has fallen in the hands of the Mongols!

Sounds of war.

Voice: The eastern walls have been demolished!

Sounds of war.

Voice: The Mongols have entered Baghdad!

Sounds of war

Voice: Duwaidar has been killed! Duwaidar has been killed!

Sounds of war

Voice: A group of young Muslims dressed in white shrouds have fallen martyrs on the bridge.

Al Mustasim: Oh God! If I had only received those Muslim youths, listened to them, and heard their advice! Instead I was amusing myself with women.

Sounds of war

Al Mustasim: I will surrender and obey! I will surrender and obey! Come on, porter, senior officer! All of you come here!

Enter the porter and the senior officer.

Al Mustasim: handing over some bags filled with money, Take this money to Holaku! Take this money to Holaku!

Exit the porter and senior officer.

Noises and voices are heard.

Holaku enters laughing scornfully.

Holaku: Oh Caliph! How could you send me a message asking me to get back after we have crossed all these vast distances without seeing you, talking together and then asking for your permission to get back home? Hahaha!, Oh Caliph, don't you know that God had selected Genghis Khan to govern the whole world and granted him and his descendants the surface from the globe from east to west? So anyone who cooperates obeys us and strengthens up heart and soul will be happy with his life, but he who opposes us will never be happy and never enjoy his life!, Oh Caliph, (scornfully) what are these large boxes?

Al Mustasim: This is my wealth! I award it to you, oh king, all of it!

Holaku: No, this is not enough!

Al Mustasim: I have nothing more!

Holaku: What about the gold that is buried in the palace courtyard?

Al Mustasim: Yes, yes, at your orders.

Holaku: addressing the Caliph, Come on, go with these soldiers and show them the gold.

Exit the Caliph with Mongol soldiers.

Holaku laughs scornfully while the boxes are opened for him one by one.

Enter the Caliph with the soldiers.

Soldier: My Lord, the whole place is full of pure gold buried in the courtyard.

Holaku: Looking at the Caliph, For what purpose did you collect all this wealth? You were supposed to use it on building up your army to safe guard you and your rule! Soldiers take him! Peel of his face skin and bring it to me!

Caliph murmurs some words.

Caliph: I want to perform ablution, I want to offer prayer! I want to perform ablution, I want to offer prayer!

Holaku: Take him away!

Caliph is dragged outside; his voice is heard uttering successive screams and then stops.

Enters one soldier.

Soldier: My lord, he died in our hands before we completed peeling off his skin.

Holaku: Even if he is dead, peel off his face's skin and bring it to me.

Holaku: Now bring along Ibn Al Algami.

Enters Ibn Al Algami, proud of his dress.

Holaku: Welcome our friend!, After making him sit near him he continues, Listen Ibn Al Algami, you have been working devotedly for us through the long past years and you have been our loyal spy. Your words and advices to the Caliph proved charming. He agreed and obeyed you in all matters and now we are going to reward you! You will be responsible for the ministry and for running all affairs in Baghdad.

Holaku looking at Ibn Al Algami, examining him closely.

Holaku: Didn't you want this?

Ibn Al Algami: My Lord, but....

Holaku: protesting, Forget about this and assume your responsibility. You will be consulting and referring all matters with the Mongol's prince, the governor.

Holaku introduces a youth.

Ibn Al Algami: amazed, This one?

Holaku: Of course yes, and I will go on to capture by force the rest of the Muslims countries up to Al Sham[1].

Holaku: pointing on to Ibn Al Algami, Once again, to war! Power is rightness and that is our everlasting slogan.

CURTAIN DROP
END OF ACT 3

1- Al Sham comprises the countries Lebanon, Syria, and Palestine.

ACT 4

Scene:

Ibn Al Algami sitting on the minister's seat while some notables are attending.

A voice from the scene says

Voice: And the day passes by.

One of the notables: Oh Ibn Al Algami, you must interfere to stop this mockery! The Caliph's graves were unearthed, their bones were dispersed and a lot of places were burned! Honorables were violated, Baghdad's library was robbed and all books were thrown into the river to form a bridge for their horses.

Enters Holaku boiling.

Holaku: Hello, dear minister! What news do you have from Baghdad?

Ibn Al Algami: Hello our great king! My Lord, all people of Baghdad are happy and looking forward to meet you, even the mistaken ones who resisted the Mongols are awaiting your forgiveness.

Holaku: Forgiveness in the form of Sultan Izz Uddeen style?

Ibn Al Algami: What is Sultan Izz Uddeen style?

Holaku: Sultan Izz Uddeen, the King of Rum, had resisted one of our leaders whom we had sent for him, and he fought against him instead of receiving him warmly. I was angry with him. A few days ago he came to the boundaries of Tabriz after he came to know that we have captured Baghdad. But the way, in which he apologized, seemed very strange. He drew a picture of his face on the bottom of a shoe and presented the shoe to me.

Holaku takes off the shoe, facing the public and raising the shoe to show that picture.

Holaku: Sultan Izz Uddeen said: The image, which I drew under your shoe is mine and I hope it may do as a mediator for me and makes me proud of your mildness, So Ibn Al Algami, don't you want me to forgive him? I forgave him.

Ibn Al Algami: My Lord, the Mongols are supposed to be punished. The citizens are complaining, because the Mongols started to attack and encroach upon them.

Holaku: You and Tulsi look quite similar in everything, even in speech. He had the same idea, when we were in Tabriz. We told him that we were in a state of occupation that forces us not to give much concern and care of people's affairs. But when we finish our occupation and conquest, then we will listen to the people's complaints and grievances.

Silence.

Holaku: I came to bid you good bye, for I am going back to the Mongol's land. So farewell, our dear friends.

Ibn Al Algami: Farewell Sir, farewell.

Holaku: with a sign to the prince he addresses Ibn Al Algami., Work in co-operation with the Mongol prince. Haha! Power is rightness and that is our everlasting slogan.

Exit the prince along with Holaku.

One of the notables: Oh Ibn Al Algami! Why didn't you tell him about what happened in Baghdad?

Ibn Al Algami: You have the answer yourself. One of the notables: Telling him that the people of Baghdad are happy! There is neither might nor power except Allah the most High, the Greatest.

Ibn Al Algami leaves his majlis, light starts to fade till complete darkness.

A voice from the scene.

Voice: And the days pass by.

Ibn Al Algami is sitting in his council with some of his assistants.

The Adhan (call for prayer) is heard.

Enters the Mongol prince.

Prince: Oh Ibn Al Algami, send somebody to silence this sound!

Ibn Al Algami: My Lord! That is Adhan, the call for prayer!

Prince: This is a mere disturbance, Ibn Al Algami, it is not Adhan.

Then turning to his assistants.

Prince: Silence him, silence him!

The prince goes near to Ibn Al Algami, Ibn Al Algami tries to get up, but the prince puts his foot on Ibn Al Algami's thigh.

Prince: No need for this! I have come to tell you that our forces killed forty thousand of the village's and now they are on their way to Al Basrah.

The man: *shouting at the minister's face*, Ibn Al Algami's son! Symbol of disloyalty and treason once again!

Turning to the audience

The man: Who knows? He may be there among you now!, Moving to the middle of the hall. Oh Arabs, oh Muslims! Kick out Ibn Al Algami out of your countries, for Holaku is coming back!

Getting down to the hall and addressing the audience.

Kick out Ibn Al Algami, symbol of treason! Kick out the symbol of treason! Kick out Ibn Al Algami!

The Baghdadi shouts at Ibn Al Alami's face

Kick out Ibn Al Algami out of your countries, for Holaku is coming back!

Getting down from the stage shouting

Kick out Ibn Al Algami out of your countries, for Holaku is coming back!

Moving through the rows looking for Ibn Al Algami and shouting

Kick out Ibn Al Algami out of your countries, for Holaku is coming back!

Repeating these words he proceeds to the door of the hall while the curtain is dropped.

COMPLETE DARKNESS
END OF THE PLAY

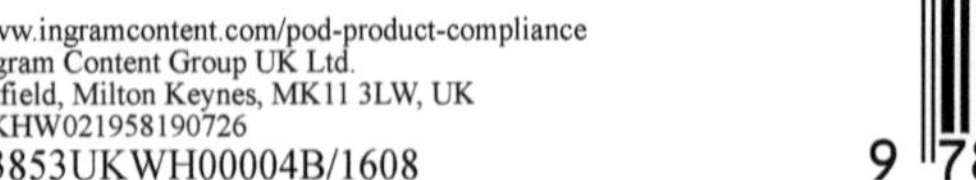

www.ingramcontent.com/pod-product-compliance
Ingram Content Group UK Ltd.
Pitfield, Milton Keynes, MK11 3LW, UK
UKHW021958190726
13853UKWH00004B/1608

9 789948 024255